T0165674

BEGINNING
KARATE

BEGINNING KARATE
by
Tonny Tulleners

©1974 TONNY TULLENERS
All rights reserved
Printed in the United States of America
Library of Congress Catalog Card Number: 74-78904

Seventeenth printing 2007

ISBN-10: 0-89750-027-X
ISBN 13: 978-0-89750-027-2

GRAPHIC DESIGN BY DAVID KAPLAN

WARNING

This book is presented only as a means of preserving a unique aspect of the heritage of the martial arts. Neither Ohara Publications nor the author makes any representation, warranty or guarantee that the techniques described or illustrated in this book will be safe or effective in any self-defense situation or otherwise. You may be injured if you apply or train in the techniques of self-defense illustrated in this book, and neither Ohara Publications nor the author is responsible for any such injury that may result. It is essential that you consult a physician regarding whether or not to attempt any technique described in this book. Specific self-defense responses illustrated in this book may not be justified in any particular situation in view of all of the circumstances or under the applicable federal, state or local law. Neither Ohara Publications nor the author makes any representation or warranty regarding the legality or appropriateness of any technique mentioned in this book.

BLACK BELT BOOKS
A Division of **OHARA** 🅟 **PUBLICATIONS, INC.**
World Leader in Martial Arts Publications

ACKNOWLEDGEMENT

My special thanks to Ed Ikuta, whose photography appears in the "Beginning Karate" series featured in KARATE ILLUSTRATED MAGAZINE and this book. His professional attitude, occasionally interrupted by his light-heartedness and clowning, made our working hours a pleasant experience.

As the book goes to press after three years of work, I'd like to take this opportunity to thank Nick Thompson and Alan Shewell, the two students who appear in the book. Both were ranked second kyu brown belt at the book's printing. Also, my thanks to Tom Serrano, who posed with me for the book's cover. I hope all of their efforts will serve to motivate other young men to undertake the study of karate.

DEDICATION

I wish to dedicate this book to the most important person in my life, my wife Lois. Her seven years of training in karate have given her a better understanding of the art than the average karate "widow". Lois was recently promoted to nidan (second degree black belt) by Mr. Takayuki Kubota.

CONTENTS

ABOUT THE AUTHOR

Tonny Tulleners was born in Rotterdam, Holland on February 5, 1944 and immigrated to the United States in 1955. As a direct result of a beating received during a confrontation with five teenagers, Tulleners began studying karate at the age of 16. Four years later, he was promoted to the rank of black belt and opened his first dojo in Pasadena, California. At the same time, Tulleners began competing successfully in karate tournaments. One of his major titles includes the middleweight crown of the prestigious International Karate Championships in 1965.

At age 21, Tonny joined the Pasadena Police Department as an undercover agent and remained at this post for four years. In 1970, he traveled to Japan as a member of the American team which placed in the First World Karate Championships held in Tokyo. In individual competition at the same event, Tulleners placed third.

When he is not involved with his karate activities, Tonny enjoys flying. Today, Tulleners owns and operates several popular dojo in the Los Angeles area.

WANT TO LEARN KARATE?

The dojo doors are open to you! Come inside and sign-up
for our special beginning karate class. Meet your instructor,
ask him questions and take your first karate lesson.

Many people who would like to study karate are hesitant about approaching a dojo because of the lack of reliable introductory information. This book is aimed at filling this information void. We will follow neophyte Nick Thompson through his first visit to a legitimate dojo, share the responses he gets to his questions, and work with him through his beginning lessons.

Tonny Tulleners, a well-known West Coast shotokan instructor, will serve as instructor to Nick Thompson. Tonny's lessons, complete with photos and detailed explanations of each move, will be geared for both the beginning student in the dojo and the student working entirely on his own at home.

Constant and determined repetition of each lesson is the key to successful home training. Practice duplicating the moves shown in the pictures until they become natural and fluid. Three-times-a-week practice of each technique is an absolute minimum. In addition, Tonny strongly recommends the use of a full length mirror to permit comparison of your form with the ideal form of the pictures.

Early lessons will deal almost exclusively with separate moves of the hands and feet essential to acquiring proper movement and coordination. In future lessons, these and more sophisticated moves will be combined into sequences and techniques. Likewise, the stances taught in the first lessons are chosen for their convenience in introducing students to the concepts of power, timing, balance and coordination as they apply in karate.

Q. I've been thinking about taking karate lessons, but I've never actually walked into a school before. May I ask you a few questions now that I'm here?

A. Sure. Have a seat. I'll try to answer any questions you might have.

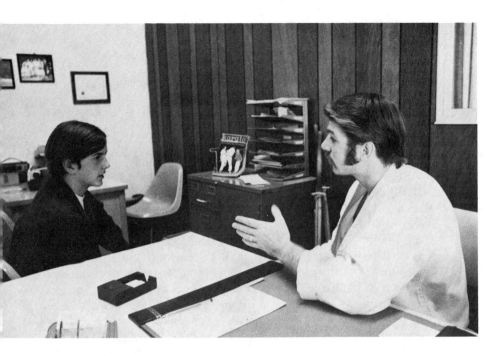

Q. First of all, what would I need to begin taking lessons? What would be expected of me?

A. Well, you ought to be in reasonably good health, but mostly it's a matter of your having a real desire to learn karate and improve yourself.

Q. What is the difference between judo and karate?

A. Judo is mostly concerned with sweeping and throwing techniques, followed by mat-work similar to the holds used in wrestling. You must have a hold on your opponent before executing a judo technique. Karate, on the other hand, consists of punching, kicking, striking and blocking techniques executed in rapid sequences.

Q. How much will lessons cost me?

A. First of all, in karate the most expensive is not always the best. I'd estimate that most dojo ask between $15 and $30 a month on a two classes per week basis, but you just can't equate price to the quality of instruction. As for equipment, the only piece that is really indispensable is the karate uniform, or gi, essential for its durability and the freedom of movement it permits. Although you'll probably want a mouthpiece and protective cup before long, the gi itself can be bought for $18 to $35.

Q. What are the chances of being injured in classes?

A. It is possible to receive an injury, but the chances are

surprisingly small since your training will be constantly supervised.

Q. Let's say I was one of the unlucky few. Would I be covered by any kind of insurance?

A. Most dojo, unless they maintain a group coverage for their students, will require you to sign a waiver before you begin attending class.

Q. Am I going to have an advantage over other beginners who are older than I?

A. Not really. You might, but in my adult classes (ages 15 to 50 plus) I frequently see the smaller or older students full of will-power and desire outperform the potentially more capable but less dedicated students. When it comes to age, the limitations are sometimes more mental than physical.

Q. How would the early training differ for a woman?

A. Surprisingly little. Naturally, I don't look for as much power from them as from a man, but the techniques are almost identical.

Q. How much should I practice at home in proportion to time in the dojo?

A. How good do you want to be? I recommend that my students, who attend one-hour classes twice weekly, at least match that at home. The really committed karate student will schedule daily workouts for himself.

Q. This sounds funny, but can I flunk out of a dojo?

A. It's not very likely, as long as it is obvious that you're making a sincere effort and are really interested.

Q. I'm confused about what seem to be "religious" aspects of karate—the bowing and meditation, for instance. Do these have something to do with Zen or Buddhism?

A. You must remember that the coordination of mind and body is the very heart of the karateka's art. He is not in prayer when you see him meditating (*mokuto*), but rather he is clearing his mind of the day's tensions and focusing his concentration on karate, thus putting himself in the right frame of mind for his training. The kneeling and bowing (*rei*), you see at the opening and close of a class are traditional gestures of respect and discipline. The ritual is solely involved with the art itself.

Q. How long will it take before I can use my karate skills with confidence?

A. Several factors would be involved, but I would estimate from six months to a year would be required before your training becomes automatic and natural. You're going to need practical experience from training with others and any real versatility simply takes time. Making sure that a student's confidence doesn't outstrip his ability is a never-ending responsibility for all sensei.

Q. How and when can I compete in tournaments?

A. Most of today's tournaments have beginner categories competition, with no real minimum training time required for participants. Personally I would recommend training at least a year before attempting to enter freestyle competition.

Q. How do I advance and how long will it take me to make black belt?

A. Advancement is determined by your success in passing promotional tests that are conducted periodically by your instructor or a board of black belts. Test requirements are usually posted in the dojo. If you fail a test, you may try again on the next test date.

Three or four years of regular training would be my estimate of the minimum time required to obtain a black belt. This would not be true, of course, for the student who could only train twice a week. As always, promotion is relative to individual potential and effort. To attain the black belt, a student must successfully advance through the lower and intermediate belt classes (*kyu*) designated by the following: white belt (9th, 8th, 7th levels), purple belt (6th level), green belt (5th and 4th levels), and brown belt (3rd, 2nd, 1st levels).

When a student earns his black belt he is elevated to the rank of *shodan* (1st degree) and begins working his way numerically up to the rank of *godan* (5th degree), the highest rank possible through active training. Black belt rankings of 6th to 10th degrees do exist, but they are essentially honorary degrees, bestowed for promoting and contributing to the arts.

Q. I've noticed some other schools around town. What's the difference between your school and the others?

A. There are many styles of karate. The style this school teaches is shotokan, which is Japanese. Shotokan is known for its aggressiveness, speed and power. Other styles, such as kempo, Korean, etc., emphasize different aspects.

LESSON 1

CLASS IS NOW IN SESSION

The upward block, punching exercises and front snap kick are covered in this lesson. These basic techniques will be integrated into more advanced techniques and sequences in the upcoming lessons. As you begin practice, emphasize constant repetition and frequent workouts. A full-length mirror is almost a necessity to effectively compare your form with that of the photographs. Finally, always take five minutes for calisthenics and general loosening up exercises before you begin your workouts.

1

A

B

C

COURTESY IN THE DOJO

Every time you enter or leave the workout area, (1) you should bow. When it is time to begin class, (A) assume the Japanese sitting position in which, through meditation, you put yourself into the proper frame of mind for training. This usually lasts about one minute and is followed by (B-C) the traditional bow, a procedure which is repeated at the end of each class. This ritual is a gesture of respect and discipline.

NATURAL STANCE

Throughout lesson one, your starting position will be the natural stance. The natural stance requires that your feet be placed approximately a shoulder-width apart. Your arms should be held relaxed in front of your body, ready for action.

UPWARD BLOCK

(1)Begin by placing your hands in the position of the completed upward block. Your right hand, now on your right hip, will execute the block and terminate in the present position of your left hand. (2)Gradually retract your left hand as your right hand moves up at an angle across your body. Be sure your blocking hand moves outside of your retracting hand and shields your entire head. (3)After your right hand passes your eyes, (4)turn it to the finished position. Your left hand should simultaneously complete its return to your left hip.

1

COMMON ERRORS

(X) The block is too far away from your head; it would probably be difficult to stop a strong punch. (Y)When the block is too close to your head, a strong punch could easily knock your blocking hand against your head. (Z)A block too high above your head wastes time and movement.

X

CLOSE UPS

(A)The proper ready position of the hand is with your fist turned upsidedown and (B) held against your waist.

A

2

3

4

Y

Z

B

APPLICATION

FRONT VIEW

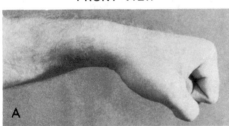

A

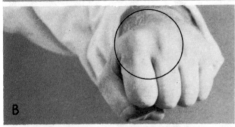

B

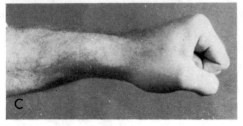

C

PUNCHING EXERCISE

(1)Begin by placing your hands in the position of the completed punch, right hand in the ready position, your extended left hand shoulder high at the center of your body. (2-3) Begin to retract your left hand to your waist while simultaneously extending your right punching hand. Note the positions of the fists as your hands pass each other. Your elbows should lightly skim the sides of your body. (4)Rotate your punching fist one-hundred-and-eighty degrees clockwise during the last three inches of the move. Do not lean with your shoulders or turn your body while punching. Make sure your punch follows the shortest distance between you and your opponent's body—a straight line.

NOTE:

(A)Notice that your fist is in a straight line with your forearm when your hand is held in the correct position for punching. (B)The proper striking area of the fist is your first two knuckles. (C)Tilting your fist upward could result in damage to fingers or wrist upon contact.

COMMON ERRORS

(X)Rotating your punching fist too soon pulls your elbow away from your body. A curved punch also results in elbow injury when extended quickly. (Y)A punch completed at the outside of your body rather than in the center results in loss of power. (Z)Reaching forward with your shoulder to strike your target will affect your balance, weaken your punch and slow down your next move. Close in on an opponent by advancing with your feet until you are close enough to attack effectively without having to reach with your body.

FRONT SNAP KICK

(1) The correct position in which to begin learning the front snap kick is with your knees slightly bent, feet together and weight distributed equally on both feet. (2) Then bring your knee up level with your waist in a cocked position, keeping your foot horizontal to the floor. (3-4) Without raising or

COMMON ERRORS

(X) Pointing your kicking foot straight up is the chief cause of toe injuries. This kick would usually swing past your opponent's body into his arms. (Y) When the snap of your leg begins before your knee is waist high, injury frequently results from striking your opponent's leg or knee. Raise your knee before starting the snap. (Z) If the heel of your stationary leg is off the ground, power and balance are lessened. Learn to judge distance so that your stationary leg will not have to move.

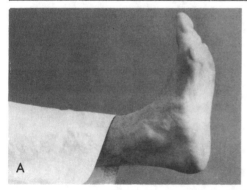
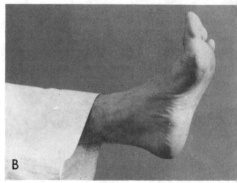

FOOT POINTING EXERCISE

Correct pointing of your foot requires continuous practice until it begins to feel natural. At first, balance yourself by holding one hand against a wall. Extend one leg parallel to the ground, as in a fully extended front kick. (A-D)

lowering your knee, quickly snap your leg to its full extension. (5) Without pausing, return it to the cocked position. Remember, your knee remains at exactly the same height during the snap. (6) Your leg does not return to the floor until the snap move is fully completed.

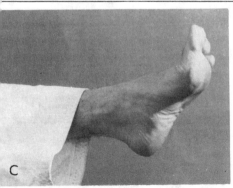
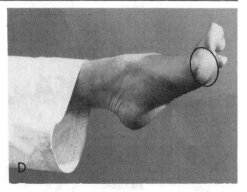

Now work your foot back and forth through the positions shown, attempting to hold the last position (D) for several seconds. The ball of the foot (circled) is the only part of your foot which should make contact when striking your opponent.

SIDE THRUST KICK

(1) Assume a natural stance with your knees slightly bent. (2) Raise the knee of your left leg straight up to your waist in a cocked position before starting any motion to the side. (3) Thrust your leg out in a straight line to your side until (4) it is fully extended. Notice that the striking area of your foot is the heel and upper edge of the foot. Your toes should be pointed down and away from the kick. (5) Retract your leg quickly to the cocked position and (6) back to the floor. Keep your arms close to your body and your stationary leg bent slightly throughout the kick.

COMMON ERRORS

(X) Your knee is too low to begin the kick. The resulting up-swinging motion will slide the kick past its target or strike your opponent's legs. (Y) Your knee is pointing toward your target. Your leg cannot thrust properly from this position, and the kick becomes more like a shove. (Z) The upturned foot and the hip turned away from the kick take all the power out of it.

2

3

5

6

TRAINING TIP

Since the beginner often lacks the balance for the side kick, you may find it helpful to use a wall for support while practicing the form of the kick.

FORWARD STANCE

In the forward stance, the distance between your front and rear foot should be two shoulder-widths, left foot approximately one shoulder-width from your right. Your front foot points directly forward at a forty-five degree angle. Your front leg should bear slightly more than half of your weight. Your rear leg must be kept straight to act as a brace. Your body should be held perfectly straight with your front leg, from foot to knee, perpendicular to the ground.

The forward stance is an aggressive stance used mainly for attacking.

two shoulder widths

one shoulder width

COMMON ERRORS

(1) There are three errors in the accompanying illustration: the heel of your rear foot is off the ground; your body is leaning forward instead of being straight; and your front leg is bent forward, causing excessive weight on that leg, which hampers movement and causes quick tiring.

1

2A

2B

MOVING INTO
THE FORWARD STANCE
FROM FEET TOGETHER

In (2A-3A), the forward stance is achieved by moving your right foot back at an angle and leaving your left foot stationary. In (2B-3B), the forward stance is achieved by moving your right foot forward and turning your left foot to a forty-five degree angle.

3A

3B

STEPPING IN
THE FORWARD STANCE

(1) Assume a forward stance with your left foot forward. (2-3) Pull your right foot up and in toward your left foot. Without hesitating, (4) bring your right foot forward and out as soon as it passes your stationary leg. (5) Continue the movement until the proper length and width is reestablished. The sliding foot does not lose contact with the floor throughout the entire movement.

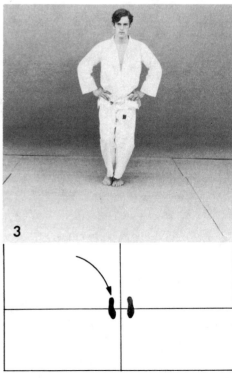

DOWNWARD BLOCK

(1) Assume a natural position with your arms in front of your body. (2) Bring your left hand upward next to your face while your right arm shifts to cover your body. (3-4) Bring your left arm down sharply and retract your right arm simultaneously to the ready position on your hip. (5) The block and the retraction are completed at the same instant. Then repeat the same block with your right arm and continue to alternate.

Use this downward block against low punches and kicks. Limit contact to the lower part of your forearm at the wrist.

COMMON ERRORS

(X) The body is left vulnerable because both arms are being held too high. (Y) Blocking with a straight elbow will often bend your elbow the wrong way on contact and result in injury. (Z) This error is avoided by keeping your elbow slightly bent, which helps absorb shock and protects your elbow.

X

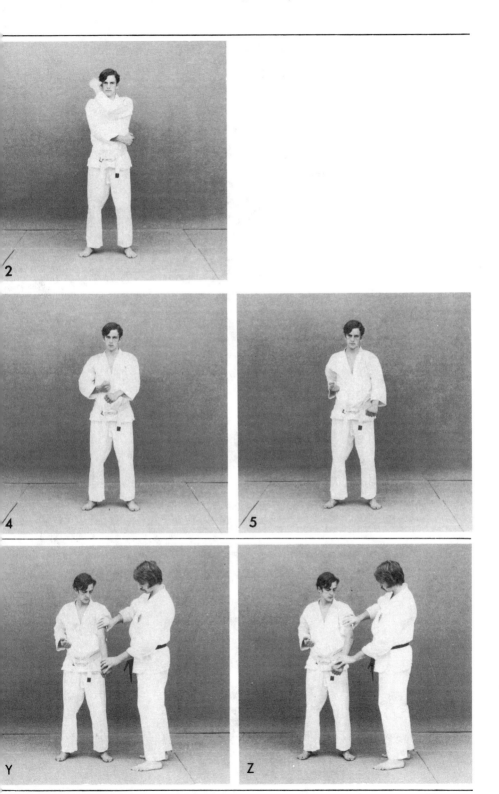

FRONT SNAP KICK
FROM
THE FORWARD STANCE

Since you will seldom have your feet together, (1) you should practice the front snap kick from the forward stance. (2-6) Pick up your right knee as before, then snap your leg out from a waist high position.

FORWARD

RETURN

7B

8B

9

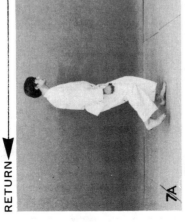

7A

8A

You can step forward from position 6 into positions 7B and 8B, or you can return to your original position, as in 7A and 8A.

Practice both ways. Remember, keep your body height the same and your stationary leg bent.

31

LESSON 3

BACK THRUST KICK

(1) Begin the back kick with your feet together. (2) Raise your left leg to about waist height and (3) locate your target. (4) Without turning your body, drive your leg straight back until it locks outward. Only the heel of your foot should make contact with your opponent. Don't let your leg bounce after it locks. Keep it straight until you pull it back in one motion to a cocked position. (5) Returning to this position before placing your foot back on the ground maintains balance. (6) Lower your leg. You are now in the proper position to repeat the kick.

COMMON ERRORS

Your body is leaning too far away from the kick. You could easily fall forward upon contact. Also, your body is turned sideways while kicking and your striking foot is in the wrong position. Never kick with the flat part of your foot.

TRAINING TIPS

Since it is difficult to maintain your balance in the beginning, it is a good idea to practice just the form of the kick by using a wall for support. In this way, it is easier to achieve good form when you later try to balance without the wall.

FORWARD PUNCH

(1) Assume a left foot forward stance with your left arm extended. (2-3) Begin the in-and-out movement that is used when stepping in the forward stance. (If necessary, see the previous lesson for how to move when in the forward stance.) (4) As soon as your right foot lands, (5) start to punch with your right hand while retracting your left hand to the ready position and (6) follow through, completing the punch.

Keep your body perpendicular to the ground and shoulders straight. Upon completion of the forward punch, your forward arm and leg should be on the same side (right arm and right leg).

COMMON ERRORS

The mistake shown here is starting the punch before finishing your foot movement. You'll be straight-arming your opponent rather than punching him if your punch is fully extended before the foot movement is completed. There is no power in this punch. Move close enough to the target before punching, not after.

two shoulder widths

one shoulder width

HALF FACING STANCE

The half facing stance is primarily defensive. Your weight distribution and length-width distribution should be the same as in the forward stance. The main differences are that your rear leg is bent (although your back foot still points at a forty-five degree angle) and your upper body and hips are turned to the front at a forty-five degree angle. This makes your body a smaller target. Most of the blocks are executed from this stance.

FRONT VIEW

STEPPING IN THE HALF FACING STANCE

(1) Assume a half facing stance with your left foot forward and your feet a shoulder-width apart. (2-3) Pull your right foot up and in toward your left foot. Without hesitating, (4) bring your right foot forward and out as soon as it passes your stationary leg. Continue the movement until the proper length and width is reestablished. The sliding foot does not lose contact with the floor throughout the entire movement.

INWARD BLOCK

(1) From the starting position, (2-3) raise your right hand to your right ear with your elbow pointing slightly to the rear. Note that your left arm doesn't move at all when this is done. (4-5) As your arm swings counterclockwise in a semi circle toward the center of your body, retract your left hand to the ready position on your hip.

Both hands should finish simultaneously. From here you can continue alternating right and left. Note that the finished position of the block is approximately located at shoulder height, with your arm held at a slight angle for proper strength. Your elbow should be about six inches away from your body.

2

4

5

1

2

OUTWARD BLOCK

(1) From the natural stance, (2) bring your hands into a preblocking position. Only your right arm can completely cover the upper half of your body from this position, so it executes the block. (3) Swing your right arm out to block while retracting your left hand to the ready position. Be sure your blocking hand passes outside your retracting

hand. (4) Both hands should complete the motion and finish simultaneously.

3

To alternate, remember that the hand on your hip which is to make the next block must travel along the belt line while your other hand covers the upper part of your body. Continue the movement without hesitation until the block is completed.

4

LESSON 4

REVERSE PUNCH

A basic weapon in every good karateka's arsenal, the reverse punch, may be executed from either the fighting stance or the half facing stance. (1) Begin by rotating your hip from the forty-five degree position into the forward stance position. (2) Start the punch with your right (rear) hand while halfway through this rotation. (3) Upon completion of the punch, return your right hand and hip simultaneously to the starting position.

Practice the entire move slowly at first, then build up speed until your return is as fast as your punch. The most critical and difficult part of the reverse punch is the rotation of your hips, from which most of your power derives. The difference between the forward punch and the reverse punch is that the latter is always executed with the rear hand or the hand opposite the forward leg.

1

2

3

FIGHTING STANCE

The fighting stance is designed to afford maximum flexibility for attack or defense. It is shorter than both the forward stance and the half facing stance. Position your forward foot approximately one-and-one-third shoulder-width in front of your rear foot and keep your feet about the width of your hips apart. Keep your weight distributed equally over both legs. Your front foot points directly forward; your rear leg points forward at a forty-five degree angle. Don't let your rear foot turn sideways.

FRONT VIEW

SLIDING

There are many uses for sliding. Besides stalking your opponent, it is helpful for closing small distances when you are on offense and for retreating when an opponent is getting too close. (1) Assume a fighting stance. (2) To slide forward, advance your front foot the required distance. (3) Then follow immediately with your rear foot. To retreat, reverse the procedure. Upon completing each slide, your stance should be approximately the same length and width as before, with your feet pointing the same way. Both feet remain in contact with the floor throughout the entire movement.

SIDE VIEW

INCORRECT

2

3

WHEEL KICK

(1) From the natural stance, (2) raise your leg parallel to the floor in a cocked position and point your knee directly at your opponent. (3) Snap your leg forward, striking with the ball of your foot. (4-5) Return your leg to the cocked position, then assume the natural stance.

It is important to keep your stationary leg bent and the foot flat on the floor while kicking. Never lift the heel of the stationary leg to get your kick higher, and never drop your knee while snapping your leg back. Be sure to bring your leg into the cocked position before dropping it to the floor.

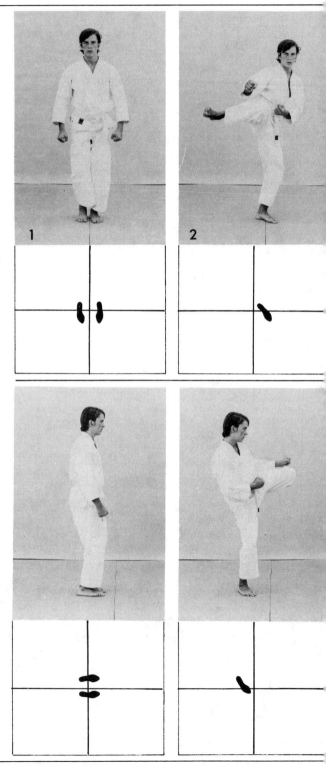

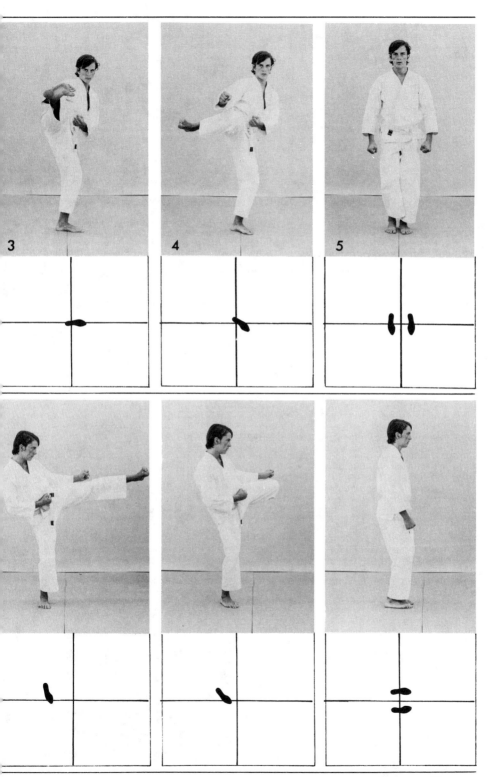

PIVOT IN
FORWARD STANCE

A pivot or turn made from the forward stance should be made as quickly and efficiently as possible. In this stance, the front leg bears sixty percent of your total body weight, so your rear leg is easier to move. (1) Assume a left foot forward stance

with your hands on your hips. (2) Bring your right leg across your body approximately two shoulder-widths and place the ball of your foot firmly on the floor. (3) Turn your hips and shift your weight accordingly, (4) then finish by facing opposite your starting direction.

3

4

PIVOT AND BLOCK

In the side view of the pivot with an added downward block, (2) notice how the arm is prepared to

4

block, but (3-4) remains in position until (5) the turn is completed, (6) whereupon it is moved down.

5

6

1

COMBINATION KICKS
(Using One Leg)

The combination kicks pictured here are governed by the same basic rules as are the individual kicks covered in the previous lessons. You must keep your stationary leg bent—foot flat on the floor—and locate your target. In the first combination, the same leg is used to make both (1-3) a front kick and (4-7) a back kick in one continuous motion.

3

6

1

COMBINATION KICKS
(Alternating Both Legs)

Photos (1-9) illustrate the same two kicks by alternating both legs. Alternate kicks are usually stronger because the weight is shifted and it is easier to maintain balance. However, they are slower than the one-leg kick because two separate motions are required.

When you have acquired the feel of these two combinations, try both the one-leg and the alternating-leg methods with the front kick and the side kick and the front kick and wheel kick. Also, try them from your fighting stances.

4

7

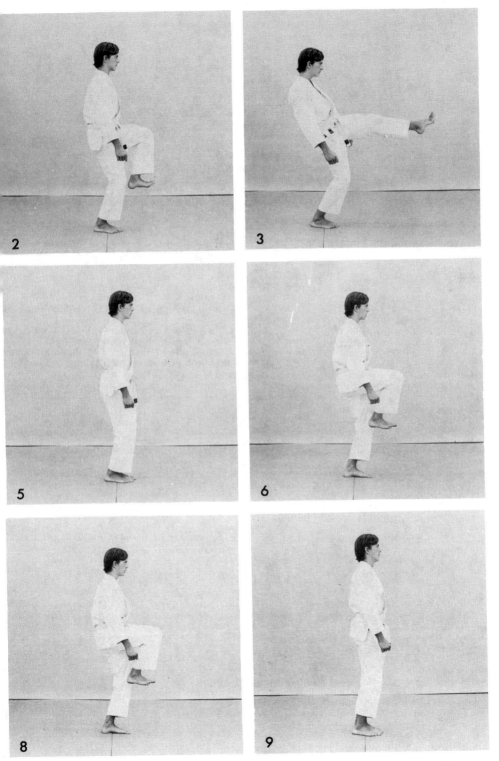

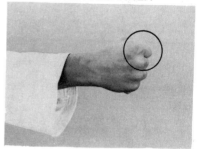

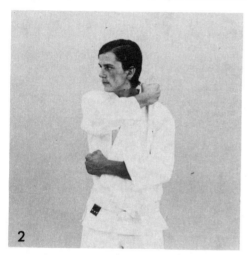

BACK FIST STRIKE

Normally used as an attack to the face, the back fist strike is fast and results in a stunning effect. (1) From a natural stance, (2) locate your target on your right and bring your right hand up to the left side of your neck while your left hand moves over to cover your right rib cage. (3) Start your right elbow in motion toward your opponent. When your elbow reaches full extension (4-5), snap your fist outward without hesitation. The prop-

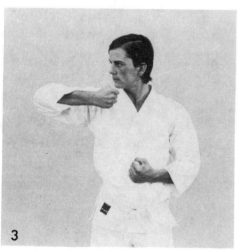

er striking area of the fist is your first two knuckles. (6) Retract your right hand back to the left side of your neck. Notice that during the delivery of the strike, your left hand is retracted to the ready position on your left hip.

IMPORTANT: Keep your elbow slightly bent during the snapping motion. Locking your arm can easily result in damage to your elbow. It shouldn't take long to discover if you are practicing the back fist incorrectly.

SLIDING
AND REVERSE PUNCH

Sliding from the freestyle stance to cover short distances was demonstrated in lesson four. Now you will apply the step in conjunction with the reverse punch. (1) Assume a left foot forward fighting stance. To strike your opponent, you must be close enough, so begin the technique by (2) moving your front foot forward until you have achieved the

3

proper range. (3) Notice the punch is not landed until after your foot has been securely planted. (4) Immediately after the punch has been fully extended, your right foot should slide up approximately the same distance as your left foot moved and (5) be followed by the retracting of your right hand. You are now in the proper position to repeat the movement.

4

5

PUNCH, FRONT KICK, PUNCH

(1) From a right foot forward fighting stance, (2) execute a left hand reverse punch. (3-4) While the punch is still fully extended, deliver a front snap kick with your left foot. (5) Bring your left foot back into the cocked position before (6) setting it down in front of you. (7) Then quickly follow up with a right hand reverse punch, (8) retract your right hand and assume a left foot forward fighting stance.

REVERSE PUNCH COMBINATION

(1) From a right foot forward fighting stance, (2) execute a left hand reverse punch. (3) At the moment the punch is fully extended, step forward with your left foot without hesitating, using a

forward stance and leaving your left hand extended. (4) As soon as your left foot lands, follow up with a right hand reverse punch. (5) Then retract your right hand and assume a left foot forward fighting stance.

LEG DEFENSE
AND COUNTER PUNCH

(1) From a left foot forward fighting stance, (2) shift all your weight to your right leg while simultaneously lifting your left leg up into a high cocked position to cover part of your upper body. Your blocking leg should not extend beyond the side of your body. Be sure to keep your stationary leg bent while momentarily balancing yourself in this position. Notice

3

that neither your body nor your hands have moved. (3) Return your left leg to its original position, (4) then follow your block with a right hand reverse punch. (5) Retreat your right hand and assume a left foot forward fighting stance. You are now in the proper position to repeat the movement.

This particular block is used mainly to defend against kicking attacks.

4

5

BACK STANCE

The back stance is used mostly for defensive purposes, and seventy percent of your body weight is supported by your rear foot. Your heels must be aligned in a straight line so your feet form a right angle, with a distance between them of about one-and-one-half shoulder-width. Because your rear leg supports the bulk of your weight, your front leg is light for easy kicking. The back stance also allows easy shifting into an aggressive forward stance.

SIDE VIEW

OPEN HAND BLOCK AND BACK STANCE

(1) From an upright position (or a natural stance), (2) step forward with your right foot, assuming a left foot back stance, and bring your right hand into a cocked position at the left side of your head. Your right hand, with the palm facing your head, should be held higher than your left hand, which covers the front of your body. (3) Once you have assumed a solid stance, begin your block and (4) complete it.

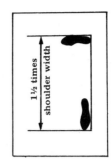

1½ times shoulder width

FRONT VIEW

3

4

The actual contact of the block is made with the knife edge of your hand. Your fingertips should be about shoulder height, with your elbow not more than six inches from your body. When the block is completed, your left hand should rest against your solar plexus in a guarding position, and your blocking hand and forearm should move through the same plane. Do not bend your wrists.

1   A   B

COMBINING THE BLOCKS

In order to develop the coordination necessary for proper defense, you should mix the order of the four basic blocks so you can perform them in any given sequence. Having an opponent on whom you can practice these blocks will help you to visualize them better. All attacks pictured here are forward punches, except for (5), which is a front kick.

(1) The attacker, A, assumes a left foot forward stance and brings his hands to the proper starting position while B, assumes a natural stance. (2) B executes the upward block, (3) the inward block, (4) the outward block, and (5) the downward block. (6) B counterpunches the attacker after executing the downward block and (7) retracts his left hand, assuming a right foot forward fighting stance.

3

6

2

4

5

7

1   A   B

BLOCKING AND COUNTER PUNCHING IN SEQUENCE

This series (1-13) contains basically the same blocks as the previous series. The difference is that after each block, the person being attacked counters with a reverse punch to various target areas, and assumes a fighting stance before executing the next block.

4

7

10

11

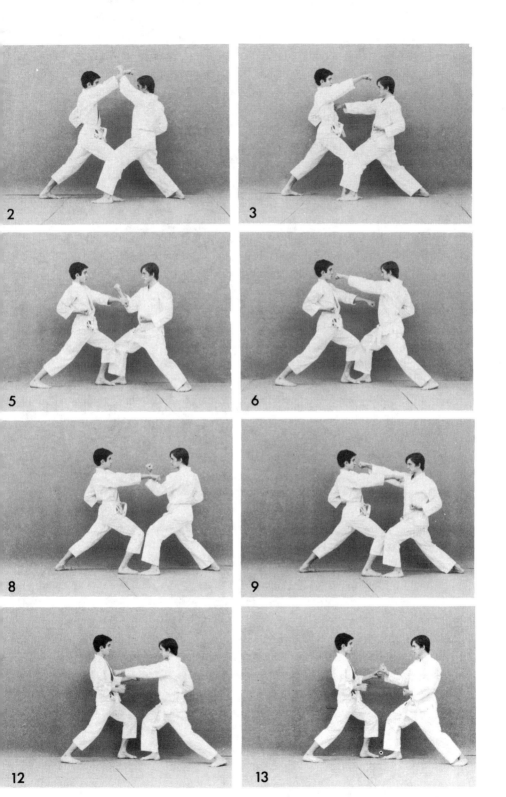

SLIDING TECHNIQUES
FOR ATTACKING

(1) From a right foot forward fighting stance, (2) *A* moves his right foot closer to *B*. (3) As soon as his right foot is securely planted, he lunge punches with his right hand, (4) while simultaneously sliding up his left foot slightly to shorten his stance. (5) By shortening the stance, he is now able to slide his right foot forward again if necessary. (6) Without pausing, he follows up with a left hand reverse punch, (7) retracts his left hand and assumes a right foot forward fighting stance. He is now in the proper position to repeat the movement.

BACKFIST COMBINATION

This combination consists of the same sliding movements as the previous sequence, but this time, (1-4) *A* starts his attack by sliding in with a right hand backfist strike. (5) Then, sliding in farther, (6) he follows up with a left hand reverse punch, (7) retracts his left hand and assumes a right foot forward fighting stance. He is now in the proper position to repeat the movement.

1

STEPPING AND SLIDING
TECHNIQUES FOR ATTACKING
(Lunge Punch, Reverse Punch)

If in doubt as to how to execute the step in the forward stance, see lesson two. (1) From a right foot forward fighting stance, (2-3) *A* steps toward the opponent and (4) executes a left hand lunge punch. In this case, *B* has stepped back to avoid the attack, so *A* has immediately followed his punch by (5) sliding his left foot closer to *B* and (6) delivering a right hand reverse punch. (7) *A* then retracts his right hand and assumes a left foot forward fighting stance.

3

6

2

4

5

7

STEPPING AND SLIDING TECHNIQUES FOR ATTACKING
(Back Fist, Reverse Punch)

This combination consists of the same stepping and sliding movements as the previous sequence, but varies in one respect. (1-4) Initially A steps forward and attacks with a left hand back fist strike, (5-6) then he follows up with a right hand reverse punch. (7) A then retracts his right hand and assumes a left foot forward fighting stance.

2

4

5

7

BASICS OF THE LEG SWEEP

Sweeping is one of the most effective ways of upsetting your opponent's balance before launching your main attack. In most instances, your opponent will be unable to counter while being swept. Properly applied, the intention of the sweep is hidden by a fake or another technique and takes the opponent by surprise. The photos in this lesson demonstrate only the actual sweep, not how to blend it into combinations.

REMEMBER: The sweep does not have to knock the opponent down to be effective.

WHERE TO SWEEP

Photos A and B show how to execute the sweep by striking with your instep as near to your opponent's ankle as possible. The higher on his leg your foot strikes, the more difficult it is to execute the sweep effectively.

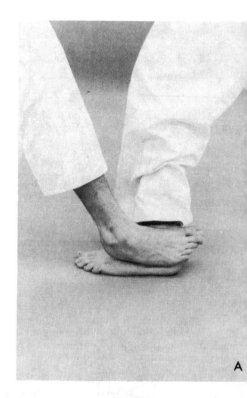

A

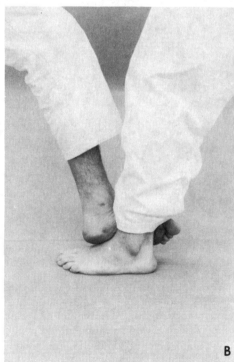

B

OUTSIDE SWEEP
(Rear Leg)

(1) The opponent and yourself are positioned in the left foot forward fighting stance. (2) Move your right leg in a circular counter-clockwise motion toward your op-

ponent's front leg. (3) Upon contact with his leg (as near to the
ankle as possible), (4) sweep his leg
outward (5-6) and then follow him
to wherever he falls or moves.

OUTSIDE SWEEP
(Front Leg)

The execution of this sweep is basically the same as the previous one, but it is executed with your front leg. Notice that the foot positions of the two fighters are opposite here. Starting from a right foot forward fighting stance, (1) move your left leg (2) to a position

4

adjacent to your front leg. (3) This move allows your right leg to be within sweeping range of your opponent's front leg. (4) Forcefully sweep his leg outward (5-6) and then stay with him so you will be in position to execute a follow-up attack.

5

6

1

2

INSIDE SWEEP

The opponent and yourself are positioned in the left foot forward fighting stance. Because you are sweeping from the inside here, your front leg will execute the sweep. (1) Move your right leg from the starting position (2) to a position adjacent to your front leg, (3) enabling that front leg to reach the opponent's front leg. (4) Again, sweep his leg forcefully outward and (5-6) follow him as he moves.

3

Always consider the possibility your opponent might see the sweep coming and attempt to avoid your sweeping leg. Using your entire body momentum in the sweep could cause you to turn too much and leave yourself open to counter-attack. So, remember, keep your body momentum to a minimum. Look back through these three sweeps and examine the body angle of the attacker in each sequence.

HOOKING
(Rear Leg)

The act of hooking an opponent's leg is normally accompanied by a pushing or shoving tactic, mainly because you are not merely breaking your opponent's balance, but moving him bodily. (1) The opponent and yourself are positioned in the left foot forward

fighting stance. From this position, (2) move your right leg in a circular counterclockwise motion (3) until it wraps around your opponent's leg above his left knee. (4) Simultaneously, straight-arm his face or torso and pull his leg toward you. (5-6) Then follow him as he falls.

HOOKING
(Front Leg)

The execution of this hook is basically the same as the previous series, but it is executed with your front leg. Notice that the foot positions of the two fighters are opposite here. Starting from a right foot forward fighting stance, (1) move your left leg (2) to a position

4

adjacent to your front leg. Again, this brings you within sweeping range of your opponent's front leg. (3) Move your right leg forward (4) until it wraps around your opponent's leg above his left knee. Again, straight-arm him forcefully as you pull his leg toward you. (5-6) Then follow him as he falls.

5

6

GRABBING ATTACK

Although I do not advise a lot of holding, there are times when such a tactic can be very effective. (1) From a left foot forward fighting stance, (2) move your left leg forward and (3) grab your opponent's front arm from the outside with your left hand. As you grasp his wrist, (4) jerk his arm sharply toward your left hip and execute a right hand reverse punch to his face. (5) Then cover your-

self.

Be sure you execute this technique in one continuous motion so your opponent has no chance to recover. It is also extremely important that you throw him off balance by pulling hard on his arm; this will render him incapable of making any attack of his own. When practicing, however, be careful not to pull your opponent so hard he falls into your punch.

COMBINATION FRONT KICK
REVERSE PUNCH

(1) From a left foot forward fighting stance, (2) switch the position of your hands and raise your right leg to the cocked position (3) to quickly deliver a front kick. After executing the kick, (4) immediately retract your kicking leg

back to the cocked position (5) and then plant it forward near your opponent. (6) Execute a left hand reverse punch to your opponent's face. (7) Retract your left hand and assume a right foot forward fighting stance.

COMBINATION WHEEL KICK REVERSE PUNCH

Follow the same sequence (1-4) for the wheel kick as that given for the front kick in the previous combination. The difference in the two combinations, of course, is in the kick itself. (5 & 6) Follow up

with a reverse punch, then (7) assume a right foot forward fighting stance.

The front kick was covered in lessons one and two, and the wheel kick in lesson four.

ELBOW STRIKES

Any time the distance between you and your opponent becomes so short that punches are no longer effective, the elbow can be used as an extremely valuable weapon. The photos describing these strikes depict five different methods of execution, all of them initiated from a half-facing horse or fighting stance. In nearly every instance, the strike may be delivered to either the face or torso, although only one target for each strike is pictured. While executing elbow strikes, keep your body perfectly straight (do not lean) and keep both feet flat on the ground. Your striking arm should be held rigid from elbow to fist with your wrist straight.

ELBOW STRIKE ACROSS

(1) From a left foot forward fighting stance, (2) slide forward with your left foot and bring

your left hand up behind your right ear. (3) Bring your elbow across, striking your opponent in the solar plexus.

ELBOW STRIKE UPWARD

(1) From a right foot forward fighting stance, (2) step forward with your right foot and begin swinging your left elbow upward. (3) Continue the motion, striking your opponent on the chin.

As you execute the upward elbow strike, your left hand should be cocked back to your left ear.

ELBOW
STRIKE BACKWARD

(1) From a natural stance with your opponent positioned behind you, (2) step back toward your opponent with your left foot and bring your left hand up behind your right ear. (3) Swing your elbow backward, striking your opponent in the solar plexus.

ELBOW STRIKE DOWNWARD

Your opponent's bent position is the result of your previous backward elbow strike. This is to demonstrate how two types of elbow strikes can be used in combination. From the final striking position in the backward elbow strike, (1) you have turned around one-hundred-and-eighty degrees counterclockwise. You should now be positioned to your opponent's right side with your right foot forward. Firmly grasp his right arm at the bicep. (2) Jerk his arm sharply toward your right hip as you raise your left elbow up to a vertical position. (3) Swing your elbow downward, striking your opponent in the back of the neck.

ELBOW STRIKE INWARD

(1) From a left foot forward fighting stance, (2) step forward with your left foot and begin swinging your right elbow inward. (3) Continue the motion, striking your opponent in the solar plexus.

As you execute the inward elbow strike, your right hand should be cocked back toward your body.

SPINNING
BACK THRUST KICK

The spinning back kick takes longer to execute than most kicks, and it forces you to momentarily turn your back on your opponent. The key to attaining success and averting disaster with this technique is making sure your opponent is off-balance or retreating (not ready or waiting) before you execute it.

(1) From a left foot forward fighting stance, (2) twist your hips clockwise and shift all your weight to your left leg. Continue the turning motion one-hundred-and-eighty degrees until your back is facing your opponent and you are looking over your right shoulder. Notice that your right leg has pulled up very close to your left but has not left the ground. (3) From this position, thrust your right leg straight back as you would with a regular back kick. (4) Then retract your right leg and simultaneously turn clockwise and face your opponent. (5) Set your right foot down, assuming a right foot forward fighting stance.

REMEMBER: Keep your stationary leg bent throughout the entire procedure.

1

3

2

4

5

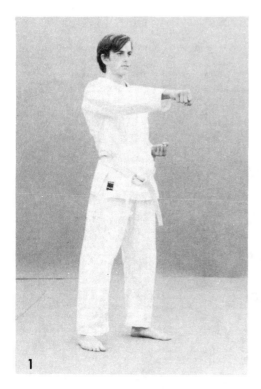

OPEN HAND STRIKES

The open hand strike (also called the shuto or knife edge strike) is used primarily to attack the head, neck and ribs. The following photos are concerned only with the hand movements of the two basic variations of the open hand strike.

INWARD STRIKE

(1) From a natural stance with your right fist clenched and extended, and your left fist held at your left hip, (2) raise your left arm (palm open) toward your left ear and point your elbow slightly toward the rear of your body. (3) Start the actual strike by moving

your elbow toward the center of your body in a circular clockwise motion. (4) As it nears the center, complete the strike by moving your left hand to a position parallel with your neck area. During the striking movement of your left hand, retract your right hand back to the ready position.

4

STRIKING ACROSS

(1) From a natural stance, (2) cross your arms by moving your left hand, palm open, to the right side of your head while raising your right hand, palm opened towards your opponent, across to your left rib cage. (3) Start the strike by moving your left elbow toward the

3

target and then (4) complete the strike by following through with your forearm. Notice that your right hand retracted to your solar plexus only as the actual strike was being completed, not while the striking hand was being brought into a ready position.

4

LESSON 10

STAMP KICKS

There are four basic types of stamp kicks. The side stamp and inward stamp are generally used to attack the knee joint, while the downward and backward stamps are specifically designed to attack an opponent on the ground.

CAUTION: Do not use the inward and side stamps to attack the knee joint in tournaments. Such attacks can cause serious injury and therefore are prohibited by tournament rules. Also be very careful when using them in practice.

SIDE STAMP KICK

(1) From a right foot forward fighting stance, (2) raise your left knee to your waist and (3) thrust your left foot downward and to the side at a forty-five degree angle. (4) Retract your leg to the cocked position and (5) return to a right foot forward fighting stance, from which you can repeat the movement. Remember to execute this attack with the knife edge of your foot.

1

3

1

SIDE STAMP KICK
(Application)

(1) As your opponent (right) moves in from the starting position to deliver a punch, (2) step to his left and (3) block his strike with your left arm. Completing the block, (4) grab your opponent's striking arm and raise your left knee to your waist. (5) Execute the stamp kick to his knee, (6) retract your left leg to the cocked position and (7) position yourself for a follow-up attack.

3

6

INWARD STAMP KICK

(1) From a left foot forward fighting stance, (2) raise your right leg to your waist and (3) stamp kick forward and across in front of your left leg at a forty-five degree angle. (4) Retract your right leg and (5) return to a left foot forward fighting stance. You are now in position to repeat the movement. Remember to execute this kick with the flat, bottom part of your foot.

1

3

2

4

5

INWARD STAMP KICK
(Application)

(1) From a left foot forward stance, (2) raise your right leg and (3) stamp kick to the outside part of your opponent's

forward knee. (4) Retract your right leg to the cocked position and (5) position yourself for a follow-up attack.

DOWNWARD STAMP KICK

(1) From a left foot forward fighting stance, (2) raise your right leg to your waist and (3) thrust it forward and down at a forty-five degree angle. (4) Retract your kicking leg to the cocked position and (5) return to a left foot forward fighting stance.

DOWNWARD STAMP KICK (Application)

When your opponent is on the ground, it is often safer to follow up with a kick rather than a punch. For example, in the following situation, a punching attack would necessitate leaning forward and making yourself vulnerable to a counterkick. From the

starting position in photo (1), (2) raise your right leg and (3) stamp kick to your opponent's midsection or groin with the heel of your foot. (4) Then retract your right foot and (5) either return to your original position or straddle your opponent and follow-up with a punch.

BACKWARD STAMP KICK

(1) From a right foot forward fighting stance, (2) raise your left leg to your waist and locate your target behind you. (3) Thrust your left foot backward and down at a forty-five degree angle. (4) Then retract your left foot to the cocked position and (5) return to a right foot forward fighting stance.

BACKWARD STAMP KICK
(Application)

If your back is to your opponent while he is on the ground, you may attack without turning. (1) Raise your left leg, (2) execute a backward stamp kick and then (3) retract your left foot.

NOTE: Be sure to execute this kick with the heel of your foot and always keep your eyes on your opponent.

COMBINATION TECHNIQUE

In this technique, the same hand is used for the first two of three attacks in the series. (1) From a left foot forward fighting stance, (2) slide your left leg toward your opponent and (3) execute a right hand reverse punch. (4) As your opponent retreats to avoid the attack, (5) step to a right foot forward fighting stance while simultaneously cocking your right hand in preparation to strike. (6) Execute a back fist strike toward your opponent's face with your right hand. When you have completed the back fist, (7) slide your right foot toward your opponent to close the distance and (8) execute a left hand reverse punch to his solar plexus. (9) Then retract your left hand and assume a right foot forward fighting stance.

HAMMER FIST STRIKE

(1) From a left foot forward fighting stance, (2) raise your right fist (3) slightly above but close to your head. (4) Throw your right fist forward and (5) down at the target, (6) making contact with the little-finger side of your fist.

A1

HAMMER FIST STRIKE
(Application)

The hammer fist strike can be directed toward your opponent's (A) neck, (B) ribs and (C) face.

B1

C1

A2

A3

B2

B3

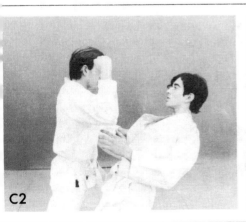

C2

C3

KNEE ATTACKS

Knee attacks are most often used in clinches when your opponent is grasping your arms, body or clothing. However, it may also be used as a finish to a combination technique if you are positioned close to your opponent.

The opponent is pictured on the right in the following photos.

ROUNDHOUSE KNEE ATTACK

(1) From a clinch, (2) raise your right (rear) leg as if you were going to execute a wheel kick. (3) Then swing your hip toward your opponent, driving your right knee in a circular, counterclock-

wise motion into his body as you pull him toward you with your hands. After completing the strike, (4) place your right foot on the floor outside your opponent's front leg and (5-6) shove him away.

FORWARD
KNEE ATTACK

(1) Again from a clinch, (2) raise your right (rear) leg as if to execute a front kick. (3) Pulling your opponent toward you with your

hands, drive your knee forward into his midsection. (4) Place your right foot on the floor between your opponent's legs and (5-6) shove him away.

UPWARD
KNEE ATTACK

(1) After blocking your opponent's reverse punch with your left hand, (2) grasp your opponent's head with both hands and pull it toward

you. (3) Drive your right (rear) knee upward—not forward—and (4) force his head down to meet it. (5-6) Then shove him away from you.

DEFENSE AGAINST A
TWO HAND SHOVE

(1) As he begins to move forward to shove you, step back with your left foot to avoid his attack. (2) When his arms are fully extended, place your hands on the inside of his wrists and (3-4) move your left hand up and your right hand down, forcing your opponent's arms wide apart. (5) With your raised left hand, (6) execute an open hand strike to his neck or head. (7) Grab him with both hands and (8) follow up with a forward knee attack with your left leg (9) to your opponent's midsection. (10-11) Then shove him away.

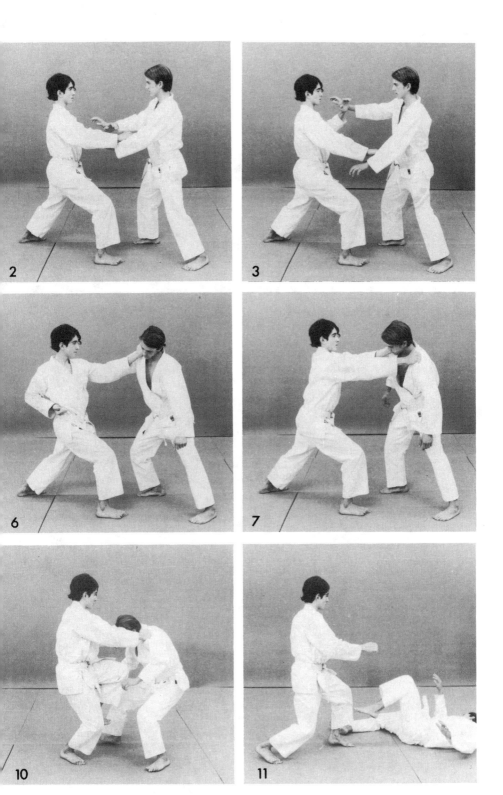

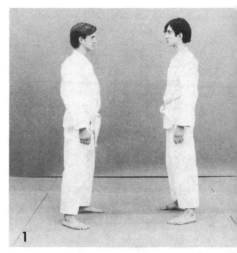

DEFENSE AGAINST GRABBING AND PUNCHING

(1) From a natural stance, (2) your opponent (right) grabs you and raises his right fist to deliver a punch. (3) Step back immediately at a forty-five degree angle away from your opponent's punching hand and cock your left hand back in preparation to block. (4) As he throws the punch, (5) execute an outward block with your left hand, similar to the open hand block shown in previous lessons. (6-7) Then immediately counter with a right hand reverse punch and (8) either cover up or execute a follow-up technique.

LESSON 12

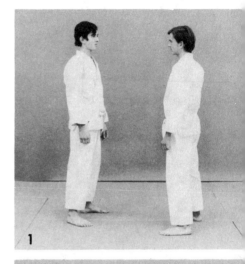

1

DEFENSE AGAINST A WRIST GRAB

(1) From a natural stance, (2) your opponent (right) reaches out and grabs your wrist. (3) Immediately grasp his extended wrist with your right hand to negate his advantage while simultaneously moving your left leg backward to adjust your distance. (4) Bring your right leg up to your waist to the cocked position and (5) execute a front kick to your opponent's midsection. (6) Then retract your right foot and (7) step forward with your kicking leg. (8) Execute a left hand reverse punch to your opponent's face and (9) cover up.

REMEMBER: Retain the grasp on your opponent's arm throughout the entire combination.

4

7

CRESCENT KICK

The crescent kick is generally used to set up a major attack. At close range, it can be used to attack the body. In the event an attacker is holding your arms from behind, the crescent kick can be used to block the punches of a second attacker. The striking area of this technique is the arch of your foot.

(1) From a right foot forward fighting stance, (2) reverse your hand position, keeping yourself covered, and direct your left foot in a circular clockwise motion toward your opponent's forward hand. (3) As the arch of your foot makes contact, (4) drive his hand away and tuck your kicking leg in toward your body. (5) Step forward and down, (6) follow with a right hand reverse punch, and then (7) cover up.

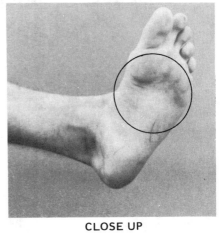

CLOSE UP

143

DEFENSE AGAINST SPINNING BACK KICKS

The spinning back kick has become a very popular technique in tournament competition the past few years. But because the user of this kick must turn his back to execute it, it is not difficult to anticipate and defend against.

MOVING AWAY FROM THE KICK

(1) Assume a right foot forward fighting stance. (2) When your opponent (right) turns, (3) move back slightly on your right foot, (4) while simultaneously raising your left leg to your waist in the cocked position. (5) When your opponent

5

6

extends his kicking leg, guide it past your raised leg with your left hand. (6) Immediately step forward with your left foot and (7) execute a right hand reverse punch. (8) Retract your right hand and assume a left foot forward fighting stance.

7

8

MOVING INTO THE KICK

(1) Assume a left foot forward fighting stance. (2) When your opponent (right) begins his turn, (3) move toward him by setting your weight on your left foot. (4) Bring your right (rear) leg forward and upward driving your knee into him as he attempts his kick, (5) knocking him off balance. (6) As soon as your feet are firmly planted, execute a right hand punch to your opponent's head and (7-8-9) follow with a left hand hammer fist strike to the back of his neck.

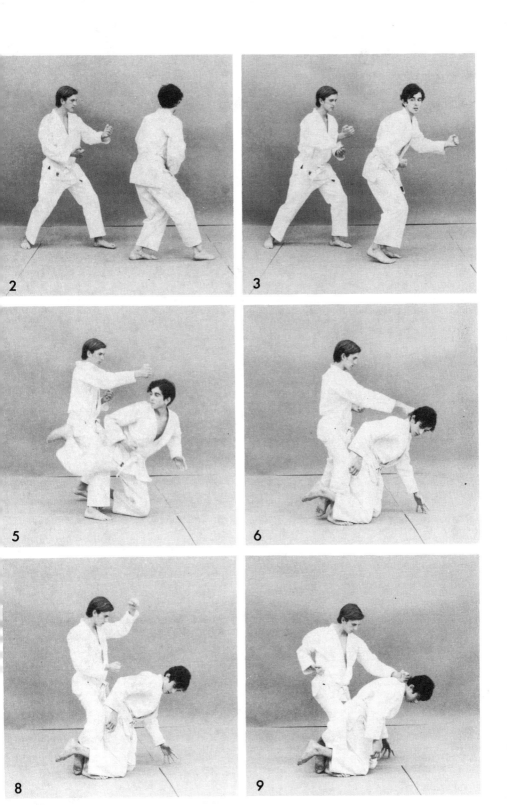

1

LESSON 13

2

DEFENSE AGAINST A FOOTSWEEP

(1) From a left foot forward fighting stance, (2) your opponent (right) fakes a punch and (3) attempts to sweep your front leg. (4) Quickly pull your left foot back toward your rear foot and simulta-

3

neously execute a left hand punch to your opponent's face. (5) Step forward with your left foot and (6) follow-up with a right hand reverse punch to his midsection. Make sure your body height is the same throughout the maneuver.

DEFENSE AGAINST
THE FOOT SWEEP
(When You Can Stay On Your Feet)

Often, a foot sweep attack will upset your balance but will not knock you to the floor. If the attacker sweeps your left leg as illustrated in photos (1) through (5), (6) quickly execute a front snap or thrust kick with your left foot before he can take advantage of your weakened position. (7-8) Immediately follow your front kick with a right hand reverse punch. (9) Retract your right hand, assuming a left foot forward fighting stance.

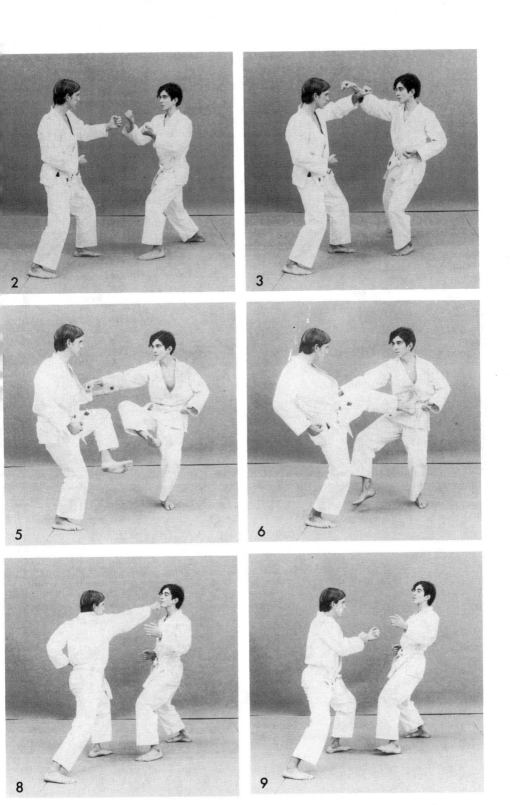

DEFENSE
AGAINST THE FOOT SWEEP
(When You Are Taken Down)

In photos (1) through (5), your opponent sweeps your front leg and upsets your balance. (6) As you fall toward the floor, (7) continue facing him so you will land on your side. (8) When he attempts to follow-up with a punching attack, (8-9) execute a wheel kick to his exposed rib cage area.

THE X BLOCK

The X block is a two handed block primarily used to stop a strong front kick attack. It may be executed from a fighting, half facing or forward stance. (1) From a left foot forward fighting stance, (2) retract both hands to your right

1

2

3

hip, (3) then thrust them forward and down with full force (4) until they are fully extended at a forty-five degree angle. Your right hand should be placed on top of your left hand when executing the X block from this side of your body.

4

APPLICATION OF
THE X BLOCK
AND TAKEDOWN

(1) Assume a left foot forward fighting stance. (2) When your opponent begins a front kick attack, withdraw your hands closer to your body. (3) When he raises his leg to kick, (4) cross your hands, right over left, and thrust them forward to stop the kick. (5) In this particular case, follow the block by turning your hands, grasping your opponent's kicking leg with both hands, and (6-7) lifting it (8) until he falls to the floor. (9) Still holding onto his leg, raise your right leg and (10) execute a stamp kick to your opponent's midsection or groin. (11) Retract your right foot to the cocked position and (12) step back, assuming a left foot forward fighting stance.

SCOOPING BLOCK AND TAKEDOWN

(1) From a left foot forward fighting stance, (2) your opponent (right) begins a front kick attack. As he lifts his leg to kick, (3) sidestep him and move slightly closer. Note the hand position. (4) While your opponent attempts to complete his kick, scoop your right arm under his kicking leg and (5) quickly bring your right (rear) leg forward. (6) Grasp your opponent across his body with your left hand and (7-8) simultaneously sweep his remaining leg with your left leg and lift him. (9-10) As he falls to the ground, (11) position yourself in a left foot forward half facing stance and (12-13) execute a right hand reverse punch as soon as he lands. (14) Retract your right hand and cover.

DEFENSE AGAINST A ONE HAND LAPEL GRAB

(1) From a natural stance, (2) your opponent (right) grabs your clothing with his right hand. (3) Immediately step back with your right foot and raise your left hand (4-5) for an inward block. (6) Continue the momentum of the block until your left hand cocks back to your right ear and then (7) execute a back fist strike. (8-9) Follow-up with a right hand reverse punch. (10) Retract your right hand and assume a left foot forward fighting stance.

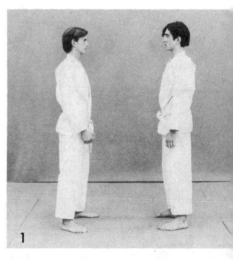

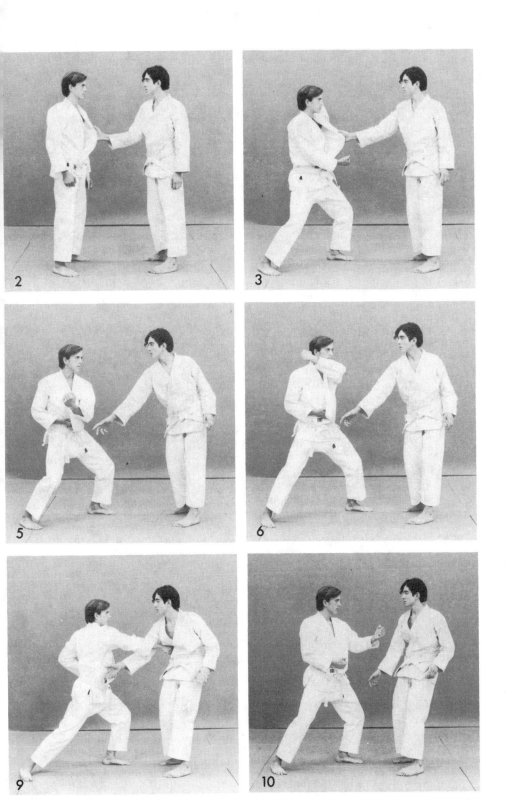

DEFENSE AGAINST A TWO HAND LAPEL GRAB

(1) From a natural stance, (2) your opponent (right) grabs your clothing with both hands. (3) Immediately step back with your right foot to a half facing stance while clasping your hands together. (4) Without hesitating, strike his forearms with your forearms (5) as you draw your hands back to your left hip. In most cases, this will break your opponent's grip. (6-7) Follow-up by striking at his throat with your clasped hands. (8) Then cover up.

LESSON 14

SHUFFLING

The purpose of shuffling is to move briefly out of your opponent's range to avoid possible attack, then instantly returning to your previous position with your opposite foot. This maneuver allows you to alternate your hands and feet effectively as you block and counter while keeping your opponent within range. The actual foot movement is simple.

(1) From a right foot forward fighting stance, (2) retract your right foot (3) until it is parallel with your rear foot (note the guideline) and simultaneously switch your hand positions. The sliding foot does not lose contact with the floor throughout this movement. (4-5) Then step forward with your left foot into a left foot forward fighting stance.

Maintain the same body height throughout the movement.

SHUFFLING
APPLIED TO THE BLOCK
AND PUNCH COMBINATION

The shuffle can be executed during blocking and countering situations. (1) From a right foot forward fighting stance, (2) retract your right foot until it is parallel with your rear foot and simultaneously begin a left hand upward block. (3) Your blocking hand should be on the side opposite your retreating foot. Complete the block as your right foot reaches your left foot, (4) then immediately step forward with your left foot. (5) Counter with a reverse punch and (6) either cover up or follow with another attack. This shuffle may be applied to any of the blocks in your repertoire.

2

3

5

6

1

SHUFFLING APPLIED
TO A COMBINATION
REVERSE PUNCH

This application may be used when your opponent is crowding you or faking an attack. (1) From a right foot forward fighting stance, (2) retract your right foot and (3) execute a left hand reverse punch. (4) Step forward with your left foot, (5) execute a right hand reverse punch and (6) either cover up or follow with a kick or a foot sweep.

4

SHUFFLING APPLIED TO THE BLOCK-PUNCH-AND-KICK COMBINATION

With a little practice, you will quickly discover that it is not difficult to blend a front kick or wheel kick with the shuffle. (1) From a right foot forward fighting stance, (2) retract your right foot and simultaneously begin a left hand inward block. (3) Complete the block as your feet come together. (4) But instead of stepping forward with your left foot this time, bring it up to your waist in the cocked position and (5) execute a front snap kick. (6) Retract your left foot, (7) step in with the same foot after the kick, and (8) execute a right hand reverse punch. (9) Then cover up. (There are numerous other applications of the shuffle but they are too complex for the beginner).

DEFENSE
AGAINST THE CHOKE

(1) As soon as your attacker (right) wraps his arm around your neck, begin your defense. (2) Grasp the wrist of his choking arm to relieve some of the pressure, and (3) simultaneously step out to your right, driving your left elbow into your opponent's solar plexus. (4) Grasp his choking arm with both hands and slip out from under it. (5) Retain your hold and pull his arm down and away from him. (6-7) With your left leg, sweep his nearest leg behind him and (7) high in the air. (8) Hang on to your opponent as he tumbles to the ground. (9) Simultaneously, position yourself for an immediate left hand reverse punch, (10-11) execute it to his face and (12) then cover up.

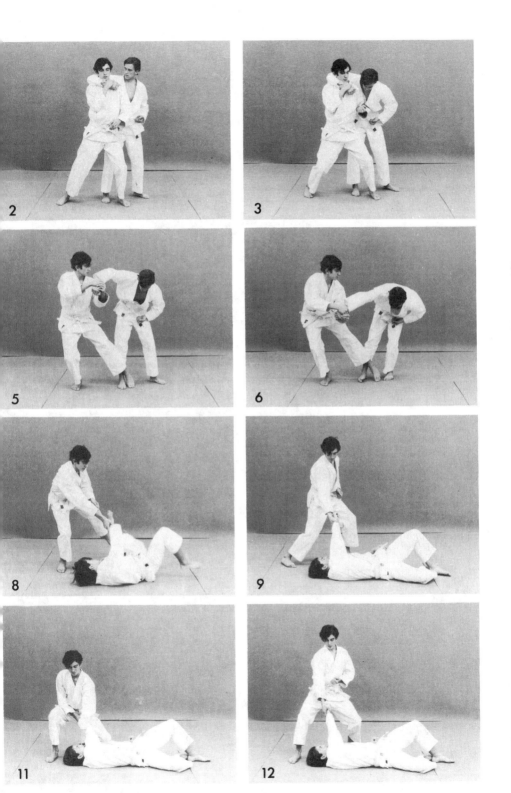

DEFENSE
AGAINST THE ARMLOCK

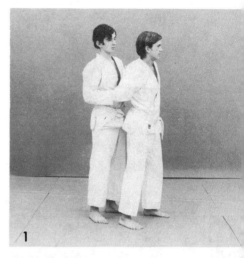

1

Unless there is a tremendous difference in size and strength between your and your attacker, it will take both of his hands to put you in an armlock. (1) As soon as your opponent attempts to apply the armlock, resist the pressure, (2) step back slightly with your left foot, and execute an elbow strike to his face. (3) Pivot clockwise on your right foot, and counter-grab either of his arms to control his movement. (4) Bring your right leg up to your waist in the cocked position and (5) execute a side kick to your opponent's midsection. (6) Retract your right leg and (7) step into your opponent as you drop your kicking leg. (8) Execute a left hand reverse punch, (9) then cover up. Note that you grasp your opponent's arm throughout most of the movement so that he will stay within striking range.

4

7

FAKING THE
FRONT KICK (High)

(1) From a left foot forward fighting stance, (2) raise your right leg quickly and forcefully into the cocked position so that your opponent will expect a front kick. If your movement is convincing, he will drop his arm for a downward block. If you hesitate long enough, he will miss with his block, leaving himself wide open for the actual kick. (3) From the cocked position, pull your leg to the side, parallel to the ground and (4) execute a wheel kick to his head. (5) Retract your right foot, (6) stepping into your opponent with your kicking foot, and (7) follow-up with a left hand reverse punch.

FAKING THE
FRONT KICK (Low)

(1) From a left foot forward fighting stance, (2) raise your right leg in the same manner as in the last sequence to lure your opponent into a downward block. When he commits himself to the block, (3)

execute a front kick to his mid-section. (4) Retract your leg to the cocked position and step into your opponent with your kicking foot, and (7) follow-up with a left elbow strike to his face.

TRAPPING OPPONENT

It is difficult to anticipate how your opponent may attack. In a fight he is unlikely to share with you his plans of how, when, where, or with what he is going to launch his attack. One of the best methods of fighting is to lead him into fighting you the way you want to be fought. Invite him to attack by leaving him an apparent opening. But don't be obvious, or you won't fool him at all.

Generally, if your opponent is able to do so he will counter any attack you make. This assumes he was able to stop your original attack. In these instances, it will be the counterattack you will be waiting for. Block his counter and attack again immediately.

CAUTION: Do not make your first attack too difficult for him to stop as this will almost guarantee his mounting an effective counterattack. The following three examples will give you some ideas on how to lead him into a counterattack you control.

INVITING A COUNTERATTACK
(A)

(1) From a left foot forward fighting stance, (2) shift slightly forward and attack your opponent with your left hand. In doing so, give your opponent plenty of opportunity to counterattack your exposed left side. (3) As your

opponent takes the bait and begins his counterattack, (4) use the same lead hand to block his counter with your forearm, and instantly (5-6) execute a right hand reverse punch. (7) Then cover or follow-up with another attack.

INVITING A COUNTERATTACK (B)

(1) From a left foot forward fighting stance, (2) start your attack with your right leg by (3) executing a front snap kick. Do not make the kick too forceful or too difficult to block. (4) As you are retracting your right foot and your opponent begins to counterattack, (5) return your kicking foot to its original starting position while you block his reverse punch with your left arm. (6-7) Instantly attack your opponent again with a right hand reverse punch, (8) then cover up or follow with another attack.

2

4

5

7

8

INVITING A COUNTERATTACK (C)

(1) From a left foot forward fighting stance, (2-3-4) again start your attack by executing a front snap kick with your right leg. In doing so, make it relatively easy for your opponent to block it. (5) As he begins to counter, (6) swiftly return your kicking leg to its original starting position. (7-8-9) Then simultaneously execute a left front snap kick and block your opponent's punch with your left hand. (10) Step toward your opponent with your kicking foot, (11) execute a right hand reverse punch, and (12) cover up.

DISTRACTIONS

In a match, numerous ways to distract your opponent present themselves. Utilize them to set him up for an effective attack. The following three examples illustrate methods of focusing your opponent's attention on an area other than the one you are intending to attack.

DISTRACTING YOUR OPPONENT (A)

(1) From a left foot forward fighting stance, (2) punch with your left hand and (3-4) simultaneously kick with your right foot. Your kick is the main attack and should be well hidden by the lead

hand punch. (5) Retract your right foot, (6) step down towards your opponent, and deliver a right hand lunge punch. (7) Then slide in with a left hand reverse punch and (8) cover up.

DISTRACTING
YOUR OPPONENT
(B)

(1) From a left foot forward fighting stance, (2) punch with your left hand while simultaneously (3-4) sweeping your opponent's front leg with your right foot. Be sure your sweep is well hidden by your lead hand punch. (5) Step down toward your opponent with your sweeping foot and execute a right hand lunge punch. (6) Follow immediately with a left hand reverse punch. (7) Grab your opponent or push with the hand that made the reverse punch. (8-9-10) Simultaneously, sweep your opponent to the ground with your left foot. (11) Move in close to your opponent and (12) execute a left hand reverse punch to his head.

DISTRACTING
YOUR OPPONENT
(C)

(1) From a left foot forward fighting stance, (2) make a high quick feint with both hands. (3) As your opponent reacts, lift your right leg and (4) crescent kick his front leg at the knee just enough to make it buckle slightly. (5) Bring your right leg up to your waist in the cocked position. (6) Without hesitating, execute a front snap kick to your opponent's midsection. (7) Retract your right foot and (8) step down toward your opponent. (9) Deliver a left hand reverse punch to his face and (10) cover up.

Bear in mind that this technique or variations of it using a crescent kick to the leg are especially effective against an opponent who likes to use his front leg to kick while you are attacking.

For our complete selection of martial arts books, videos and DVDs visit our Web site
www.blackbeltmag.com

BLACK BELT BOOKS
A Division of OHARA PUBLICATIONS, INC.
World Leader in Martial Arts Publications

BLACK BELT
MAGAZINE · VIDEO

BOOKS

TAO OF JEET KUNE DO by Bruce Lee
BEST SELLER

small-circle **jujitsu**
by wally jay

OKINAWAN GOJU-RYU II
Advanced Techniques of Shorei-Kan Karate
by Seikichi Toguchi

SPECIAL FORCES/RANGER-UDT/SEAL HAND-TO-HAND COMBAT/ SPECIAL WEAPONS/ SPECIAL TACTICS SERIES
KNIFE FIGHTING, KNIFE THROWING FOR COMBAT
by Michael D. Echanis

VIDEOS

BLACK BELT MAGAZINE PRESENTS
NUNCHAKU
KARATE WEAPON OF SELF-DEFENSE
By Fumio Demura
VHS VIDEO

BLACK BELT
MAGAZINE VIDEO PRESENTS
Rape Awareness & Prevention for WOMEN
"If you happen to anyone, anyplace, at any time."
Features: Bill Wallace, Barbara Hale, Robert Ferguson
A VIDEO PRESENTATION OF A POSITIVE PRODUCTION

BLACK BELT
MAGAZINE VIDEO PRESENTS
TAI-CHI CHUAN by Marshall Ho'o
BBMV 103

BLACK BELT MAGAZINE PRESENTS
Bruce Lee's Fighting Method
Basic Training Skill in Techniques
performed by Ted Wong, Richard Bustillo
A MARTIAL ARTS INSTRUCTIONAL VIDEO

DVDs

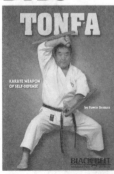
TONFA
KARATE WEAPON OF SELF-DEFENSE
by Fumio Demura
BLACK BELT

The Art of the **NINJA** Volume 1
by Jack Hoban
BLACK BELT

PRACTICAL AIKI-DO VOLUME I
by Robert Koga
BLACK BELT

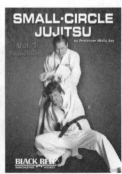
SMALL-CIRCLE JUJITSU
by Professor Wally Jay
Vol. 1 Foundations
BLACK BELT

To receive our complete catalog call 1-800-423-2874 ext. 10